A YOUNG READER'S GUIDE
TO
SHAKESPEARE'S *A MIDSUMMER NIGHT'S DREAM*

A YOUNG READER'S GUIDE TO SHAKESPEARE'S *A MIDSUMMER NIGHT'S DREAM*

MARIA FRANZISKA FAHEY

Maria Franziska Fahey is the author of *Metaphor and Shakespearean Drama: Unchaste Signification*, which was shortlisted for the 2012 Shakespeare's Globe Book Award. She is a member of the faculty at Friends Seminary, where she has taught English for more than twenty-five years.

Copyright © 2019 by Maria Franziska Fahey

All rights reserved.

Except for the use of brief quotations in a book review, no part of this book may be reproduced in any form by any electronic or mechanical means without the express written permission of the author.

First Printing, 2019
Second Printing, 2020, includes corrections and minor revisions of the text.

ISBN-13: 978-0-578-51138-2

ISBN-10: 0-578-51138-X

Accabonac Press
61 Jane Street, Suite 17C, New York, NY 10014

Cover illustration and design by Lauren Simkin Berke

CONTENTS

Preface vii
    Using Your "Imaginary Forces" to Read a Shakespeare Play vii
    Using This Guide x
    Other Helpful Guides xi

Before You Begin 1
    Finding Passages by Act, Scene, & Line Numbers 1
    Some Old-Fashioned Words Worth Knowing 3
    Reading Shakespeare's Figures of Speech 5
        Metaphor & Simile 5
        Metonymy & Synecdoche 10

Guiding Questions—Scene-by-Scene 11
    Act 1, Scene 1 11
    Act 1, Scene 2 25
    Act 2, Scene 1 29
    Act 2, Scene 2 40
    Act 3, Scene 1 47
    Act 3, Scene 2 53
    Act 4, Scene 1 68
    Act 4, Scene 2 79
    Act 5, Scene 1 82

Larger Questions 93

Appendices 94
    1. Listening to the Rhythms of Shakespeare's Poetry: An Introduction to Meter 94
    2. On How an Edition of *A Midsummer Night's Dream* Is Made: Quartos & Folios 99

Acknowledgments 101

PREFACE

Using Your "Imaginary Forces" to Read a Shakespeare Play

In Shakespeare's time the way people learned a story or the news was quite different than in ours. Think of stories you know from your favorite shows and movies, or think of how you learn the news: talk is accompanied by photographs, movies, and images that add to whatever words someone is speaking. On social media people post photographs and videos along with their written messages. And photographs accompany written news in newspapers and magazines. Of course, many of us still read books without pictures, but nowadays, we learn most stories by seeing images along with hearing or reading words. Shakespeare lived more than 400 years ago, from 1564-1616, a time when there were no photographs or movies and many fewer pictures available than now. Printed books were precious and very expensive. Most people gained access to information and entertaining stories through spoken language. Part of the fun, and also the challenge, of reading a Shakespeare play is having to transform words into visual images for ourselves—as people regularly did during Shakespeare's time.

When Shakespeare was writing his plays, theaters were not as fancy as ours. Plays were performed for the public in outdoor theaters without lighting, scenery, or special effects and with few props. Shakespeare knew that what he could show on stage was limited, and he knew that he was asking his audiences to imagine what the actors described as they spoke on stage. In his play about King Henry the Fifth, a Chorus speaks to the audience about the play before the first scene begins. The Chorus admits that the play cannot bring King Henry himself or "the vasty fields of France" into the theater and asks the audience members to let the play work on their "imaginary forces." The Chorus encourages them to use their imaginations to see, in their minds' eyes, the things they will hear characters talk about: "Think, when we talk of horses, that you see them, / Printing their proud hoofs i'th' receiving earth." Our "imaginary forces" make it possible to see full, moving pictures when we hear (or read) a play's words—in this example, galloping horses, leaving hoof-prints in the ground. Shakespeare relied on his audiences to listen carefully and to use their imaginations to picture scenes for themselves.

A Shakespeare play is largely talk—a series of conversations among a cast of characters. However, the talk of a Shakespeare play is often more difficult to understand than ordinary speech because Shakespeare crafted it to bring a whole world before our eyes—and to give clues to actors who would perform the roles. The series of questions in this guide is designed to help you listen carefully to what characters say so that you can use your "imaginary forces" to see the world of *A Midsummer Night's Dream* for yourself. As you read the play's language and begin to envision its world, keep in mind that the language of the play is different from that of ordinary speech. Here are a few of these differences:

✺ **Poetic Language.** The conversations in a Shakespeare play are no ordinary conversations: they were crafted by a poet-playwright who also used sound, rhythm, and imagery to tell his stories. Shakespeare often wrote in verse, so you will find that parts of the plays are printed like a very long poem.[1] In *A Midsummer Night's Dream* a young man, Lysander, tries to persuade Helena that he no longer loves Hermia. Consider the lines he speaks:

> Content with Hermia? No. I do repent
> The tedious minutes I with her have spent.
> Not Hermia but Helena I love.
> Who will not change a raven for a dove? (2.2.118-21)

In ordinary speech, someone would likely say, "I do repent the tedious minutes *I have spent with her. I love Helena, not Hermia.*" But Shakespeare's word order allows the lines to rhyme—"repent" with "spent" and "love" with "dove," giving those pairs of words special emphasis. Furthermore, the last time Lysander spoke in rhyming lines, he was proclaiming his love for Hermia. His speaking to Helena in the way he formerly spoke to Hermia accentuates his change of heart.

✺ **Vocabulary.** Written over 400 years ago, Shakespeare's plays are known for their unusually large vocabularies, including many words that were, at the time, new to the English language—some probably made up by Shakespeare himself! Almost all readers find the vocabulary of a Shakespeare play challenging to understand, but they also discover that the words Shakespeare chose often carry particular meanings important for the play.

Keep in mind that some words' meanings are not the same today as they were 400 years ago and that other words used then are rarely heard any more. Consider, for instance, the word *sinister* in an announcement about the crack or "cranny" in a wall through which lovers speak:

> And this the cranny is, right and sinister,
> Through which the fearful lovers are to whisper. (5.1.172-3)

Here *sinister* means "on the left side," which is rarely how we use the word today: now *sinister* usually means "evil."

Another word whose most common meaning has changed is *translated*. Consider what Quince says to Bottom after Puck magically turns Bottom's head into an ass's head. (*Thou* is an older word for "you.")

> Thou art translated! (3.1.120-1)

---

[1] You can find an explanation of verse and more information on the kind of poetry in the play on pages 94-98.

Although nowadays the word *translate* usually refers to turning one language into another, in Shakespeare's day, *translation* could refer to transformation more generally—in this case turning a man's head into an ass or donkey's head!

As you read the play, be sure to consult the notes in your copy of the play and to keep a good dictionary at hand, one that provides older meanings of words. (You can check your library's print or online version of *The Oxford English Dictionary* ("*OED*") which is the most comprehensive English dictionary, the one from which I provide definitions throughout this guide.) But don't feel like you have to look up every unfamiliar word. You can learn a great deal about a word you don't understand by examining nearby words you do understand. In other words, *context* can help you read unfamiliar words. Consider the word *changeling* in Puck's description of the disagreement between the Fairy Queen Titania and the Fairy King Oberon:

> For Oberon is passing fell and wrath
> Because that she, as her attendant, hath
> A lovely boy stolen from an Indian king;
> She never had so sweet a changeling.
> And jealous Oberon would have the child
> Knight of his train, to trace the forests wild. (2.1.20-5)

How could you figure out what a *changeling* is? *Changeling* refers to the "lovely boy" whom Puck claims Titania has stolen, "the child" whom Oberon wants for his train. Thus, a *changeling* must be a stolen child. (The *Oxford English Dictionary* defines *changeling* as "A child secretly substituted for another in infancy; a child supposedly left by fairies in exchange for one stolen" (*OED* 3).)

❈ **Descriptions that Provide Context.** Although Shakespeare's theater included costumes and some props, it did not include sets or lighting. (The use of electricity was centuries away, and plays were performed at The Globe, an open-air theater, in the mid-afternoon.) Audiences would have to discover important context from the characters' speeches. For instance, in act 2, scene 1, Oberon describes the place where Titania sleeps:

> I know a bank where the wild thyme blows,
> Where oxlips and the nodding violet grows,
> Quite overcanopied with luscious woodbine,
> With sweet musk roses, and with eglantine.
> There sleeps Titania sometime of the night,
> Lulled in these flowers with dances and delight. (2.1.257-62)

Nowadays such a scene could be shown to a theater audience through stage and lighting design. Thus, contemporary playwrights usually don't write such descriptions into characters' speeches, and contemporary audiences don't have to decipher and picture them.

☀ **Implied Action.** Unlike stories or novels, most plays don't have a narrator who tells us what characters are doing as they speak to each other. Playwrights can indicate specific actions with stage directions, but Shakespeare's plays have relatively few. Instead, the dialogue itself gives clues about characters' actions. Consider the following exchange when Lysander suddenly wants to be free of his former beloved Hermia. (*Thou* and *thee* are older forms of "you.")

Lysander	Hang off, thou cat, thou burr! Vile thing, let loose,	
	Or I will shake thee from me like a serpent.	
Hermia	Why are you grown so rude?	(3.2.270-3)

Lysander's telling Hermia to "Hang off" and "let loose" lets us see that Hermia is physically hanging onto Lysander as he rudely rejects her. Imagining the world of a Shakespeare play depends, in part, on listening for clues to characters' actions. Try acting out a scene with some friends and listen for clues to what your character is doing physically.

Learning to see the world of a Shakespeare play by reading or hearing its language takes some work and some patience. However, paying close attention to the play's language will give you access to the most interesting, complicated, and surprising aspects of the plays. As we heard from the Chorus in *Henry the Fifth*, Shakespeare invited and relied on his audiences to see the worlds of his plays, and Shakespeare gave us extraordinary language from which to form pictures in our minds. There are always many ways to imagine a phrase, line, or scene, but it's important to start with accurate observations of the play's language.

Using This Guide

A series of questions for each scene will help you to observe the sometimes complex and dense language accurately and to figure out what characters are saying to each other. Before trying to answer the questions for a particular scene, read through the entire scene aloud. Or, better yet, gather some friends, take parts, and read the scene aloud together. Don't be shy: you might mispronounce a word or need to read some lines slowly, but you will have a much better chance of understanding the lines when you read them aloud—and you likely will have more fun. Then, read through the scene again slowly, answering the questions as you go. If you don't fully understand a question, copy down the phrase or line that you suspect contains the clues for its answer. Once you reach the scene's end, return to those questions to see if you have been able to figure out anything further.

There are a few recommended exercises before you begin. The first is about finding passages in the play with act, scene, line numbers—rather than page numbers. The second introduces some old-fashioned words that are helpful to know. And the third introduces you to metaphors and similes: you'll encounter many of them in *A Midsummer Night's Dream*. If you

already know about any of these topics, you can skim the section and exercises quickly before you begin to read and answer questions about each scene.

Every so often some information is marked "✂ Extra ✂" (or, if a question, marked "✂ Extra Opportunity ✂") and is enclosed in a box. If you're short on time, you can skip those boxes and still come away with a basic understanding of the topic or scene.

You may find that some questions include terms or methods unfamiliar to you. For instance, an "✂ Extra Opportunity ✂" question may ask you to "scan the meter" of a line. Don't worry: you will find the necessary background information and examples in one of the sections called "appendices" at the very end of this book. You may find it helpful to read through the appendices before you begin to answer the questions. Or you may consult them when you arrive at a question that requires your knowledge of the information they provide.

Other Helpful Guides: Scene Summaries, Audio Recordings, & Performances

In the Folger Shakespeare Library edition of *A Midsummer Night's Dream*, you'll find a brief summary of the main events of each scene at the start of the scene's notes. You may be able to understand what the characters are saying and doing without reading a scene summary, but you may find it helpful to have a general sense of the plot before you read each scene. If, after reading the scene's summary and reading the scene aloud by yourself or with friends, you continue to have trouble understanding what the characters are saying to each other, locate an audio recording of the play with a cast of experienced Shakespearean actors. (Many libraries have them available, and some are available on the internet.) Read along as you listen to the audio recording of the scene you are working on. Hearing trained actors speak the characters' lines will likely help you understand much of what the characters are saying. Keep in mind that the way an actor speaks a line depends on that actor's interpretation of it and that you might have another interpretation.

You might also enjoy seeing a performance of the play, and doing so will clarify much about it. Check to see if there is a live performance at a nearby theater or borrow a film of the play from your library. If you wait to see a performance until after reading the play, you will be able to compare the way you have imagined the play-world to the way a particular director has. If you see the performance before you've read the play, be aware that the particular director's vision of the play is not the only possibility. If you watch two or more performances, look to see how different directors and actors interpret the play.

BEFORE YOU BEGIN

You will have an easier time answering the questions for each scene if you start off knowing a few things: 1. how to find a passage by its act, scene, and line numbers, 2. the meanings of some old-fashioned words, and 3. some basics about metaphors and similes. The three following sections aim to prepare you. Depending on what you know already, you can spend as much or as little time as you need on each section.

1. Finding Passages by Act, Scene, & Line Numbers

Novels tend to be divided into *chapters*, but plays are divided into *acts* and *scenes*. Because page numbers vary depending on the edition of the play, Shakespeare scholars refer instead to act, scene, and line numbers so that readers can find a passage no matter the particular edition. Usually you can find the act and scene numbers across the top of each page. In most editions you will find every fifth line number printed from top to bottom along each page's right or left margin.

Quotations in this guide are taken from the edition of *A Midsummer Night's Dream* edited for The Folger Shakespeare Library by Barbara Mowat and Paul Werstine and published by Simon and Schuster in 2016. Below is a diagram showing where you can find act, scene, and line numbers in the Folger edition. You'll see that the play is printed on the right side with scene summaries and notes on the left. If you are reading another edition, notes may be printed along the bottom and the line numbers may be slightly different.

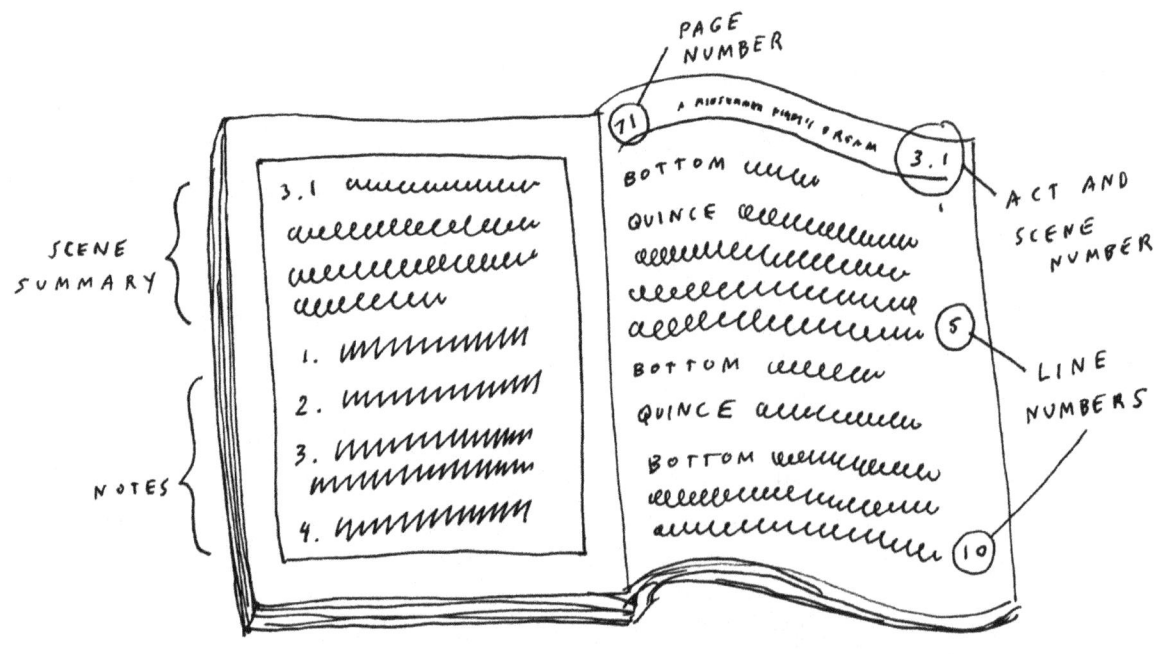

L. S. Berke

Here's an example of how to indicate the location of a line from *A Midsummer Night's Dream*. At the start of act 4, scene 1, on line 7, Bottom orders, "Scratch my head, Peaseblossom." (If you have the Folger edition, you will find it on page 121.) You could quote and "cite" (indicate) the line:

> Bottom orders, "Scratch my head, Peaseblossom" (4.1.7).

Notice that a period separates the act, scene, and line numbers, which are enclosed in parentheses.

Try one! Find Oberon's line at the start of act 3, scene 2. (It's on page 83 of the Folger edition.) Fill in the act, scene, and line numbers below:

✍

> Oberon observes, "Here comes my messenger" (____ . ____ . ____).
>   act scene line

Sometimes you'll want to refer to more than one line. At the start of act 2, scene 2 on lines 7 and 8 (page 53 of the Folger edition), Titania orders:

> Sing me now asleep.
> Then to your offices and let me rest.

Here's how you quote and cite these lines:

> Titania orders, "Sing me now asleep. / Then to your offices and let me rest" (2.2.7-8).

Notice that a forward slash (/)—called a "virgule"—marks where one line ends and the next begins and that both lines "7-8" are cited.

Try one! Find Theseus's lines at the start of act 5, scene 1. (They are on page 143 of the Folger edition.)

✍

> Theseus declares, "The lunatic, the lover, and the poet / Are of imagination all compact" (____ . ____ . ____ - ____).
>   act scene   lines

2. Some Old-Fashioned Words Worth Knowing

Throughout this guide, I provide meanings of words that are no longer as common as they were in Shakespeare's day. Since you'll come across some old-fashioned words repeatedly, it will help to become familiar with them before you start.

❊ An Old-Fashioned Pronoun—Thou, Thee, Thy, Thine

Although nowadays the only second-person pronoun we use is "you," in Shakespeare's day people had two choices—"you" or "thou." Notice that the pronoun "you" has three forms: *you*, *your*, and *yours*. "Thou" has four forms: *thou*, *thee*, *thy*, and *thine*. (In case you're interested in grammar, I've listed the name of the form in parentheses.)

old-fashioned	current	(grammatical name)
thou **Thou** givest me a present.	*you* *You give me a present.*	(subject pronoun)
thee I give **thee** a present.	*you* *I give you a present.*	(object pronoun)
thy She gives me **thy** phone number.	*your* *She gives me your phone number.*	(possessive adjective)
thine I give her **thine**.	*yours* *I give her yours.*	(possessive pronoun)

Try them! Fill in the blank with the correct old-fashioned pronoun—thou, thee, thy, or thine.

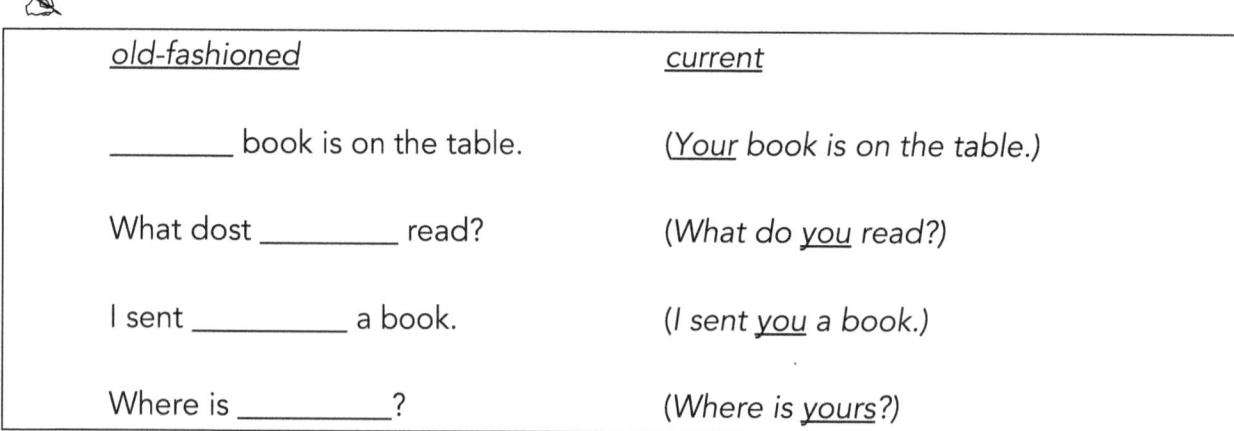

old-fashioned	current
_____ book is on the table.	(*Your book is on the table.*)
What dost _____ read?	(*What do you read?*)
I sent _____ a book.	(*I sent you a book.*)
Where is _____ ?	(*Where is yours?*)

3

❄ Other Old-Fashioned Words & Contractions

anon: at once

ere: before

e'er: ever *(Notice that the consonant "v" is removed and replaced with an apostrophe.)*

o'er: over

mark: notice, pay attention. *(Nowadays, we would say "Look!" rather than "Mark!")*

sooth: truth

sprite: spirit

translate: change, transform

would: I wish

Try using these words! Fill in the old-fashioned word that best fits each sentence below. (You'll need all but two from the list above.)

Once I found a fairy _____ hiding in my room. I was so frightened by the sight of it that I was _____ed into a quivering coward. Since then, _____ I go to sleep, I check under the bed and all _____ my room. _____ that sprite never had appeared! If _____ I see that sprite again, I shall call the fairy-catchers _____.

3. Reading Shakespeare's Figures of Speech: Metaphor & Simile

Shakespeare's plays are famous for their metaphors and similes, which are rich in meaning and sometimes difficult to understand. You'll have lots of practice with them as you answer questions about the metaphors and similes in each scene. Before you start, it will be helpful to be familiar with what makes metaphors and similes different from other kinds of speech and with a few techniques for understanding them.

"A rose is a flower" is not a metaphor. A rose is **LITERALLY** a flower. Anyone could find this out by looking up "rose" in a dictionary.

"Love is a rose" is a metaphor because it demands that we imagine how love is like a rose. A metaphor can be understood as true only if taken **FIGURATIVELY**.

※ A **METAPHOR** asserts that one thing is another thing and demands that we imagine how it can be so.

One way to analyze a metaphor is to sort its TENOR and VEHICLE.[2]

※ The **TENOR** is the subject of the metaphor—what the speaker is talking about.

※ The **VEHICLE** is what is imagined for comparison to illuminate some part of the tenor.

In the metaphor "love is a rose," *love* is the tenor and *rose* is the vehicle. The combination of the vehicle and tenor prompts you to recognize that you're hearing or reading a metaphor because the statement would be otherwise absurd or impossible. In ordinary, "literal," speech, love is a feeling, and a rose is a flower, and in literal speech a feeling can't be a flower. However, the interaction between the tenor (love) and the vehicle (rose) produces the metaphor's meaning as it challenges us to imagine what love shares with a rose.

> ⇜ EXTRA ⇝ Our English word *metaphor* is borrowed from Greek. "Meta" means *trans-* or *across*, and "phor" means *port* or *carry*; thus, *metaphor* can be translated as *transport*. The metaphor "love is a rose" transports a *rose* from the world of gardening to explain something in the world of feelings, namely, *love*. Metaphors explain something in one world by transporting something from a distant world for comparison.

---

[2] *Tenor* and *vehicle* are terms coined by I. A. Richards in 1936 for his book *The Philosophy of Rhetoric*.

Here's an example of a metaphor from the opening of one of Shakespeare's poems, Sonnet 68:

> Thus is his cheek the map of days outworn,

When we read this line, we realize that a literal cheek cannot also be a literal map, and so we know that either we're reading nonsense or we're reading a metaphor. Here *cheek* is the tenor—what the speaker is talking about—and *map* is the vehicle—what the speaker has transported from the world of diagrams, paper, and ink to describe "cheek" by comparison.

Sometimes it is helpful to sort the metaphor's vehicle and tenor in a chart:

vehicle	:	tenor
map	:	cheek

And sometimes it's helpful to sketch the metaphor, trying to show both its vehicle (cheek) and its tenor (map). Here is an example:

G. Minette

❈ A **SIMILE** asserts that one thing is "like" or "as" another thing and demands that we imagine how.

"Lucinda is like her grandmother" is not a simile. It is a **LITERAL** statement.

"Lucinda is like a hurricane" is a simile. It is a **FIGURATIVE** statement.

Of course we may have to figure out how Lucinda is like her grandmother, but comparing Lucinda and her grandmother—who both are human, female, and family—doesn't demand that we use our imagination to find similarities in altogether different categories of things as we must if we are to understand how a human being can be like a storm.

Like metaphors, similes work by comparison, but with the word *like* or *as*, similes indicate their comparisons more explicitly. Similes announce the relationship between the tenor and vehicle more directly and formally.

Let's take an example of a simile from *A Midsummer Night's Dream* spoken by the Duke to a young woman, Hermia. Hermia's father wants his daughter to marry Demetrius, but Hermia refuses. When her father brings Hermia before the Duke to complain about her disobedience, the Duke instructs Hermia:

To you your father should be as a god, (1.1.47)

When the Duke advises Hermia to obey her father or suffer the consequences, he speaks a simile that transports *a god* to describe her *father*. You could chart the simile:

vehicle	:	tenor
a god	:	father

You also could include the "you" of "To *you* your father should be as a god" and think about what the simile implies.

vehicle	:	tenor
a god	:	father
___?___	:	you—daughter (Hermia)

If her father "should be as a god," then, we can reason, she (the daughter) should be like a worshipper of that god who obeys the god's commands without questions.

vehicle	:	tenor
a god	:	father
worshipper	:	you—daughter (Hermia)

✎
Try making a drawing of this simile that combines the vehicle "a god" with the tenor "father." You may wish to include the tenor "daughter" and the implied vehicle "worshipper."

A simile names both tenor and vehicle—the father and the god—and makes clear the relationship: the Duke says that Hermia's father should "be as" a god to her. The metaphor that opens Sonnet 68 likewise names both tenor and vehicle—the cheek and the map—and makes clear their relationship: the cheek "is" the map. Sometimes, however, a metaphor does not name both tenor and vehicle. Or sometimes a metaphor does not state so clearly how the vehicle corresponds to the tenor. Such metaphors require more interpretation. Consider, for example, Helena's complaint about her beloved Demetrius's change of heart.

> For, ere[1] Demetrius looked on Hermia's eyne[2],   [1]ere=before [2]eyne=eyes
> He hailed down oaths that he was only mine;   (1.1.248-9)

We know that Helena speaks a metaphor because Demetrius cannot have *hailed down oaths* literally—only the sky or the gods could hail down hail! But Helena doesn't say explicitly what corresponds to Demetrius's having "hailed down" oaths.

We can start interpreting the metaphor by charting:

vehicle	:	tenor
hailed down (hail)	:	?

Then, we can make a logical interpretation based on the context of Helena's statement and a particular quality of the vehicle, namely, *hail*. Often more than one interpretation is possible.

If we were thinking about how when it hails, many ice balls fall from the sky, we could say:

vehicle	:	tenor
hailed down (hail)	:	spoke (oaths) too numerous to count

Or, if we were thinking about how hail can make a big noise and impression when it falls, we could say:

vehicle	:	tenor
hailed down (hail)	:	spoke (oaths) with great emphasis

Or, if we were thinking about how being hit by hail can hurt (physically), we could say:

vehicle	:	tenor
hailed down (hail)	:	spoke (oaths) that hurt (emotionally)

Part of the fun of interpreting a metaphor or simile is imagining all the various qualities of the vehicle and deciding which ones best apply to the tenor.

❦ EXTRA ❦ Two Other Figures of Speech: Metonymy & Synecdoche

Whereas metaphor and simile work by comparison, metonymy and synecdoche work by being closely related to or part of what they stand for.

※ One thing standing for another associated thing is called **METONYMY**.

> Robin (Puck) uses metonymy when he petitions the audience, "Give me your hands, if we be friends" (5.1.454). *Hands* are closely related to clapping, so "give me your hands" stands here for applause.
>
> Robin also uses metonymy when he discovers the Athenian workers rehearsing their play and asks, "What hempen homespuns have we swagg'ring here" (3.1.76). *Hempen homespun* is a homemade, coarse cloth from which the workers' garments are made. Robin calls the men by the rustic, homemade clothes they wear.
>
> Theseus uses metonymy when he tells Hermia that her choice of husband, Lysander, is "wanting your father's voice" (1.1.56). A *voice* is used for speaking, so "wanting your father's voice" here stands for her lacking ("wanting") her father's spoken agreement.

※ Part of a thing standing for the whole thing is called **SYNECDOCHE**.

> Theseus speaks a synecdoche when he says, "The lover, all as frantic, / Sees Helen's beauty in a brow of Egypt" (5.1.10-11). A *brow* is part of a *face*, and a face is part of a woman. Theseus is saying that the lover sees Helen's beauty in the face of an Egyptian woman.

The difference between *being related to* and *being part of* can be very slim, so it can be difficult to decide whether to call a figure of speech metonymy or synecdoche. The difference between metonymy and metaphor, however, is larger and more significant. In order to understand a metaphor or simile you need to imagine how a tenor in one world compares to a vehicle from a distant world: you need to imagine how one thing *is* or *is like* another thing with which it ordinarily is not associated. Metonymy and synecdoche, in contrast, are from the same world as the things they stand for.

GUIDING QUESTIONS—SCENE-BY-SCENE

A note on Greek names: For A Midsummer Night's Dream Shakespeare borrowed names and settings from ancient Greek myths. "Theseus," for instance, is a mythical king of Athens, and "Hippolyta" is the mythical Amazon queen whom Theseus conquers and brings back to Athens. Although Shakespeare set his play in ancient Greece with mythical Greek characters, he also included many aspects of his own Judeo-Christian, English world. For instance, Hermia can choose to be a nun if she refuses to marry Demetrius, and the woods outside of "Athens" are inhabited by local English fairies.

ACT 1, SCENE 1

1. The first scene begins with Theseus speaking to Hippolyta about their upcoming wedding—their "nuptial hour" (1.1.1). How is Theseus feeling about his marriage to Hippolyta?

    First, quote two phrases with clues to how Theseus is feeling:

    Then, say what each phrase reveals about how he is feeling:

2. Reread 1.1.7-11 ("Four days will quickly . . . Of our solemnities"). What does Hippolyta say about the wedding in response to Theseus? What seem to be her feelings about it?

3. What does Theseus order Philostrate to do (1.1.12-15)? (Key line: "Stir up the Athenian youth to merriments.")

4. Explain what we learn from Theseus about how he courted ("wooed") Hippolyta: "I wooed thee with my sword, / And won thy love doing thee injuries" (1.1.17-18). How did Hippolyta become Theseus's bride-to-be?

5. What does Theseus say about how, in contrast, he will wed Hippolyta?

6. Egeus brings before the duke (Theseus) a "complaint" against his daughter Hermia. Reread his speech ("Full of vexation come I . . . according to our law / Immediately provided in that case" (1.1.23-46)) as you answer the following questions:

   a. Who has Egeus's "consent" to marry Hermia? (*Consent* means "permission.")

   b. How, according to Egeus, has Lysander "bewitched the bosom" of Hermia (1.1.28)? (*Bosom* is another word for "breast"—where one's heart is.) What has Lysander been doing? What has he been giving to Hermia?

c. How, according to Egeus, has Lysander "filched" his daughter's heart (1.1.37)? (*Filched* means "stolen.") Fill in the blank with the word Egeus uses:

"With _____ hast thou filched my daughter's heart."

d. What does Egeus's choice of words describing what Lysander has done to his daughter—*bewitched, filched*—suggest he thinks about Hermia's relationship with Lysander?

e. What does Egeus name as the two possibilities for how he should be allowed to "dispose" of his daughter (1.1.43)? Fill in the blank:

"either to this gentleman / Or to her _____" (1.1.44-45)

To which "gentleman" does Egeus refer?

f. Review Egeus's entire speech. What does his complaint reveal about his idea of a father-daughter relationship?

7. Theseus advises Hermia:

   > To you your father should be as a god,
   > One that composed your beauties, yea, and one
   > To whom you are but as a form in wax
   > By him imprinted, and within his power
   > To leave the figure or disfigure it. (1.1.48-52)

   a. What does Theseus's first simile ("your father should be as a god") imply about how Hermia should respond to her father's wishes?

   b. What does his second simile (which begins "To whom you are but as a form in wax") imply about what her father has the power to do to her? Before you begin your answer, think about the qualities of *wax*. What would it be like to "imprint" a form into wax?

8. Theseus tells Hermia that the man she wants to marry (Lysander) is "wanting"—lacking—her "father's voice." What does Theseus mean? Explain in your own words Theseus's reason that Hermia must consider Demetrius a "worthier" gentleman than Lysander (1.1.55-7).

9. How does Theseus respond to Hermia's wish, "I would my father looked but with my eyes" (1.1.58)? (In this sentence *would* means "wish.") Fill in the blank:

   "Rather your eyes must with his _____ look" (1.1.59).

   In your own words, explain what Theseus is telling Hermia:

10. Theseus tells Hermia that if she refuses to wed Demetrius, she either will have to be put to death or become a nun. Theseus asks Hermia to consider if she can "endure" the life of a nun" (1.1.72). What does Theseus go on to emphasize about the life of a nun? Start your answer by quoting three key words in his description.

11. Consider the metaphor with which Theseus contrasts the life of a nun and a married woman:

> But earthlier happy is the rose distilled
> Than that which, withering on the virgin thorn,
> Grows, lives, and dies in single blessedness. (1.1.78-80)

Distilling a rose into perfume preserves the essence or scent of a rose long after the flower is dead. What does the metaphor imply about how a married woman can preserve her essence? (What could a married woman leave behind that would remind people of her even after she dies?) Fill in the tenor for the vehicle "rose essence or perfume." *(For explanations of vehicle and tenor, see pages 5-6.)*

vehicle	:	tenor
rose	:	woman
distilled	:	married
withering on the thorn	:	remain a virgin nun
(rose essence/perfume)	:	(_____)

How, then, does Theseus try to convince Hermia that marrying Demetrius is better than becoming a nun?

12. Hermia announces her decision:

    > So will I grow, so live, so die, my lord,
    > Ere¹ I will yield my virgin patent up   ¹*ere=before*
    > Unto his Lordship whose unwishèd yoke²   ²*yoke=a device fitted to an animal so that it can pull a plow*
    > My soul consents not to give sovereignty³. (1.1.81-4)   ³*sovereignty=supreme authority or rule*

    What is Hermia's decision about marrying Demetrius, the man her father has chosen for her?

    > *Extra Opportunity* — Notice the words with which Hermia describes marriage. Explain what the word "yoke" or "sovereignty" implies about Hermia's understanding of a woman's relation to a man she marries.

13. Lysander asserts that he is as qualified as Demetrius to be Hermia's husband—if not more so. What does Lysander include on his list of qualifications? What, finally, does he say "is more than all these boasts can be" (1.1.105)?

14. Make a comic strip that illustrates what Demetrius, Lysander, and Egeus say. Include Hermia, Theseus, and Hippolyta in your illustrations as needed. Stick figures are fine!

Demetrius	Relent, sweet Hermia, and, Lysander yield
	Thy crazèd title to my certain right.
Lysander	You have her father's love, Demetrius.
	Let me have Hermia's. Do you marry him[1].
Egeus	Scornful Lysander, true, he hath my love;
	And what is mine my love shall render him.
	And she is mine, and all my right of her
	I do estate[2] unto Demetrius. (1.1.93-100)

[1] *Do you marry him=You marry him!*

[2] *estate=give*

Panel 1: Relent, sweet Hermia

Panel 2: and Lysander yield / Thy crazèd title to my certain right.

Panel 3: You have her father's love, Demetrius.

Panel 4: Let me have Hermia's. Do you marry him.

Panel 5: Scornful Lysander, true, he hath my love;

Panel 6: And what is mine my love shall render him. / And she is mine, and all my right of her I do estate unto Demetrius.

15. Of what does Lysander accuse Demetrius before calling him a "spotted and inconstant man" (1.1.112)?

16. Theseus confesses that he has heard about Demetrius's relationship with Helena and says that he would have spoken to Demetrius had he not been "full of self-affairs" (1.1.115). If the "self-affairs" of which Theseus speaks are related to his own up-coming wedding to Hippolyta, what does he suggest is the effect of wooing and love on doing one's job—in this case Theseus's doing his job as duke?

17. *Extra Opportunity* After hearing the conflict over Hermia's engagement, Theseus asks Hippolyta, "What cheer, my love?" (1.1.124). Imagine what Hippolyta might have been feeling or thinking as the complaints were spoken. Then either write the private diary entry Hippolyta might write that evening, or write a stage direction describing what Hippolyta does in response to a specific line. (Be sure to indicate at what line you would insert the stage direction.)

18. Review the conversations so far (1.1.23-129). Quote one or two key phrases that reveal each character's idea of how marriage should be arranged and partners determined. Be sure to consider what each character claims (or implies) is his or her privilege or right.

   Theseus

   Egeus

   Hermia

   Lysander

   Demetrius

19. Review your list and write down one or two disagreements expressed about marriage:

20. Reread the exchange below and notice how Hermia and Lysander speak a kind of duet. Hermia continues her beloved Lysander's metaphor of the "roses" of her cheek fading. Underline the words Hermia uses to extend or develop this metaphor that likens her face to a garden of roses.

>   *Lysander*   Why is your cheek so pale?
>   How chance the <u>roses</u> there do fade so fast?
>   *Hermia*   Belike for want of rain, which I could well
>   Beteem¹ them from the tempest² of my eyes.   (1.1.130-3)   ¹beteem=grant or give
>   ²tempest=storm

21. Lysander declares that tales and history suggest that "The course of true love never did run smooth" (1.1.136). What reasons does Lysander then give to explain why not (1.1.137-51)? Jot down two:

22. Hermia responds that if "true lovers" always have been "crossed," or blocked, from being together, "Then let us teach our trial patience" (1.1.154). What is Hermia's attitude toward their "trial" or difficulties?

23. What solution does Lysander propose to their forbidden marriage? How does Hermia respond to Lysander's proposal?

24. ⚭ *Extra Opportunity* ⚭ When Hermia agrees to sneak away from her father and Athens to marry Lysander, she swears by "Cupid's strongest bow" and "the simplicity of Venus' doves" (1.1.172-4). (Cupid is the god of love, and his mother Venus the goddess of love.) But Hermia also swears by "that fire which burned the Carthage queen" and by "all the vows that ever men have broke" (1.1.176-8). (The Carthage queen, Dido, kills herself when her lover Aeneas, "the false Trojan," left her.)

   a. What do you notice about this list of love stories by which Hermia swears to leave her home to escape with her beloved?

   b. How do you feel about Hermia's running off with Lysander when you hear this list? If you were her friend, what would you ask her? What advice would you give her?

25. Helena rejects Hermia's calling her "fair" and complains, "Demetrius loves your fair" (1.1.185). (*Fair* can mean beautiful.) Explain what Helena means when she concludes:

    Were the world mine, Demetrius being bated¹,   ¹*bate*="to omit" or "except" (*OED* 7)
    The rest I'd give to be to you translated². (1.1.194-5)   ²*translate* ="to transform" or "to change in form, appearance" (*OED* III.4).

26. Helena tells Hermia,

    > O, teach me how you look and with what art
    > You sway the motion of Demetrius' heart!" (1.1.196-7)

    What might Helena mean by "how you look"? Give two possibilities.

27. If you were Helena, how would you feel when your friend Hermia tells you that she and Lysander "will fly this place" (1.1.208)—that she is leaving Athens forever?

28. Consider Hermia's description of her life before and after seeing Lysander:

    > Before the time I did Lysander see
    > Seemed Athens as a paradise to me.
    > O, then what graces in my love do dwell
    > That he hath turned a heaven unto a hell. (1.1.209-12)

    Why might Athens have seemed a "paradise" before Hermia saw Lysander? How might Lysander's "graces" have "turned a heaven unto a hell"? What does Hermia suggest about being in love?

29. Once alone, Helena speaks about Demetrius and about the nature of love. Reread Helena's speech at 1.1.232-57 ("How happy some o'er other some can be! . . . To have his sight thither and back again"). Then answer the following questions from Helena's point of view:

   a. Why does it not matter that "Through Athens I am thought as fair as she" (1.1.233)?

   b. Explain what love can do: "Things base and vile, holding not quantity, / Love can transpose to form and dignity" (1.1.238-9).

   c. With what organ of the body does "Love loo[k]" (1.1.240)?

   d. What oath had Demetrius made to Helena before he "looked on Hermia's eyne" (1.1.248)? (*Eyne* means eyes.)

   e. What does Helena expect Demetrius will do when she tells him of Hermia's flight or escape?

f. Explain Helena's reasoning in the passage below.

> And, for this intelligence¹   ¹*intelligence*=information
> If I have thanks, it is a dear expense.
> But herein mean I to enrich my pain,
> To have his sight thither and back again. (1.1.248-51)

Act 1, Scene 1 Character Review.

For each character listed below jot down a line or phrase that you think particularly reveals what each is like. (Be sure to note the line number!)

Hermia

Lysander

Demetrius

Helena

ACT 1, SCENE 2

Read through the entire short scene in which Peter Quince is organizing a play to be performed for (Duke) Theseus and (Duchess) Hippolyta's wedding. Read aloud and, if possible, with friends who each take a part. Then, answer the following questions.

1. Although Quince seems to be in charge of organizing and casting the play, how does Bottom behave? Start your answer by quoting two of Bottom's key lines or phrases.

2. For each man gathered to rehearse the play, jot down a key phrase or two that particularly reveals that man's character. Note to whom the line is said. *(As an example, I've chosen one line for Quince the carpenter.)*

   <u>Quince, the carpenter</u>

   to Bottom: "No, no. You must play Pyramus" (1.2.53).

   <u>Bottom, the weaver</u>

   <u>Flute, the bellows-mender</u> (A *bellows* is a tool that produces a blast of air to help ignite a fire.)

Starveling, the tailor

Snout, the tinker (A *tinker* mends pots and other metal household items.)

Snug, the joiner (A *joiner* makes cabinets and furniture by joining wood.)

3. Notice the occupations of the men who will be in the play. What do their jobs have in common?

4. List two or three specific differences you notice between the way these men speak and act and the way the lords and ladies in the first scene speak and act.

5. Quince worries that if Bottom were to roar "too terribly," he "would fright the Duchess and the ladies" (1.2.72-3). What must Quince imagine about the ladies for whom they will be performing?

6. Why does Quince arrange for them to rehearse "in the palace wood" (1.2.97-8)? Clue: "for if we meet in the city, we shall be dogged with company and our devices known" (1.2.99-100). About what is Quince concerned?

7. Bottom misuses certain words by speaking a word that sounds like one that would correctly fit the meaning of the sentence. Bottom's mistakes are often funny! (See how many you can find!) Consider the mistake underlined below and explain what makes it funny.

   "We will meet, and there we may rehearse most obscenely and courageously" (1.2.103-4).

   Obscenely means "offensively, repulsively, horribly; indecently" (*OED*). Bottom likely means *seemly*, which means "Fittingly, appropriately; decently" (*OED* 2).

☀ Act 1 Favorites ☀

Jot down your favorite phrase or line from act 1—either scene 1 or 2. It could be a line you just like the sound of!

Jot down a phrase or line from act 1 that brings some picture to your mind. Then make a quick sketch of the picture you see.

ACT 2, SCENE 1

Please note:
- *This scene includes a number of detailed descriptions of the fairy and human worlds. At the end of this scene's questions, you will be invited to illustrate one such description. As you work through the scene, keep your eyes open for details that bring the scenery vividly before your eyes.*
- *Robin is also called "Puck." This guide follows the Folger edition, which uses "Robin," but if you're reading another edition, he might be called "Puck."*

1. Read the Fairy's response to Robin (Puck) aloud and listen to the way it sounds (It starts, "Over hill, over dale," and ends, "In those freckles live their savors" (2.1.2-13)). What do you notice? How do the sounds (the rhythm and rhyming) of the Fairy's speech make the Fairy seem different from the couples or the workers we met in act 1?

2. ⚡ *Extra Opportunity* ⚡ Listen to the rhythms of the Fairy's response to Robin and scan the pairs of lines below. *(I've scanned the first line for you. For a full explanation of how to scan a line of verse, see appendix 1 on pages 94-98.)*

    ⏑ ⏑ / ⏑ ⏑ /
    Over hill, over dale,

    Thorough bush, thorough brier,   (2.1.2-3)

    What is the name of this meter?

    Those be rubies, fairy favors;

    In those freckles live their savors.   (2.1.12-13)

    What is the name of this meter?

3. Robin tells the Fairy that the king (Oberon) will "keep his revels here tonight" (his partying) and warns the Fairy to be careful not to let the queen (Titania) come "within his sight" (2.1.18-19). What explanation does Robin give about why the king Oberon is so angry—"passing fell and wrath" (2.1.20)?

4. The Fairy then recognizes Robin as "that shrewd and knavish sprite / Called Robin Goodfellow" (2.1.34-5). (*Knavish* means "mischievous" or playfully naughty; *sprite* is a alternate word for "spirit.") For what kind of mischief is Robin Goodfellow, also called "Puck," known (2.1.35-42)? Quote one key phrase:

5. ⚜ *Extra Opportunity* ⚜ Robin declares himself "that merry wanderer of the night" and announces, "I jest to Oberon and make him smile" (2.1.45-6). Consider the examples of his jesting (joking) Robin recounts. For instance, he "neigh[s] in likeness of a filly foal" and lurks in a bowl "In very likeness of a roasted crab" (2.1.48-50). If Robin can neigh like a horse and hide in a bowl like a crab, what special ability does he have?

6. Of what does Titania accuse Oberon at 2.1.66-75 ("But I know / When thou hast stolen away. . . joy and prosperity")?

7. Of what does Oberon accuse Titania at 2.1.76-83 ("How canst thou thus . . . Ariadne and Antiopa")?

8. Titania points out that she and Oberon have not "since middle summer's spring" met "To dance [their] ringlets to the whistling wind" (2.1.85-9). Reread 2.1.91-117 ("Therefore the winds, piping to us in vain . . . By their increase now knows not which is which"). What does Titania say is happening in the natural and human world as a result of the disturbance between the queen and king of the fairy world? Quote two or three key phrases.

9. How does Titania explain why she refuses to part with the "little changeling boy" for whom Oberon begs (2.1.127-42)?

10. What had Robin said about how Titania came to have the boy? (Look back at 2.1.21-2.)

11. Whose story—Titania's or Robin's—seems more believable to you? Why?

12. After Titania exits with her train of fairies, what does Oberon announce he will do to her?

13. Oberon orders Robin to fetch him a special flower: Oberon once saw "the bolt of Cupid" fall on it (2.1.171-2). (Cupid is the god of love.) What special power does the juice of the flower now have (2.1.176-8)?

14. ✺ *Extra Opportunity* ✺ How long does Robin say it will take him to "put a girdle round about the Earth" (2.1.18102)? (A *girdle* is a belt.)

Make a sketch of Robin putting a "girdle round about the Earth."

15. After Robin exits, Oberon says he will "drop the liquor" of the flower in Titania's eyes (2.1.185). What does he imagine Titania might look at next and "pursue it with the soul of love" (2.1.189)?

16. Oberon plans to remove the charm with another herb but only after he makes Titania give up the boy—"render up her page" (2.1.192). Explain the reasoning behind Oberon's plan to acquire the boy Titania said she has promised to keep. What does Oberon think will happen to Titania when she, under the influence of the magic juice, is pursuing some creature with "the soul of love"?

17. When Oberon hears someone approaching, he announces, "I am invisible, / And I will overhear their conference" (2.1.193-4). Write a specific stage direction for how Oberon should perform being "invisible." Feel free to suggest more than one possibility.

18. As Demetrius pursues Hermia, he says, "And here am I, and wood within this wood" (2.1.199).

    A *wood* is "a collection of trees . . . smaller than a forest" (*OED* n.1, 2a). In Shakespeare's day, *wood* also could mean "out of one's mind, insane," "reckless, wild," or "violently angry or irritated" (*OED* adj.1, 2a, 3b).

    Fill in each blank with your own words that explain what Demetrius means by each "wood":

    "And here am I, and _____ within this _____."

    What does Demetrius imply about the effect on him of his passionate pursuit of Hermia?

19. Reread Helena's response to Demetrius's order that she follow him no more:

> You draw me, you hard-hearted adamant!
> But yet you draw not iron, for my heart
> Is true as steel. Leave you your power to draw,
> And I shall have no power to follow you. (2.1.202-5)

Make a small sketch of Helena's metaphor of Demetrius as an "adamant" (a magnet) that "draw[s]" (or pulls) her heart of steel.

20. Helena continues with another metaphor. Reread the extended metaphor and complete the chart of its vehicle and tenor.

> I am your spaniel[1], and, Demetrius,
> The more you beat me I will fawn[2] on you.
> Use me but as your spaniel: spurn[3] me, strike me,
> Neglect me, lose me; only give me leave
> (Unworthy as I am) to follow you. (2.1.210-14)

[1] spaniel=a kind of dog
[2] fawn=to show delight or fondness (OED 1a)
[3] spurn=reject hatefully

vehicle	:	tenor
spaniel	:	_____
beat me	:	_____
fawn on (wags tail)	:	_____
_____	:	you (Demetrius)

What might be Helena's tone of voice when she speaks this extended metaphor that begins, "I am your spaniel"? Try performing it aloud and list two or three possibilities. Which tone would you choose if you were performing the part of Helena? What in the play leads you to this choice?

21. Consider what Helena says about the difference between women and men in love.

>   We cannot fight for love as men may do.
>   We should be wooed[1] and were not made to woo. (2.1.248-9)

[1] woo=to court, to try to win the love of

Briefly explain what Helena says.

Does Helena fit her own idea of how women should behave in love? Explain how or how not.

36

22. ᗜ *Extra Opportunity* ᗜ Helena says that in following Demetrius she will "make a heaven of hell" (2.1.250). How does Helena's remark compare to what Hermia has said about Lysander: "O, then, what graces in my love do dwell / That he hath turned a heaven unto a hell!" (1.1.211-12)? Review these two moments, and compare the situations and remarks.

23. Oberon planned to "overhear" Helena and Demetrius's "conference" while "invisible" (2.1.193-4). After they exit, for whom does Oberon express sympathy—Helena or Demetrius? Quote and cite the line from which you derive your answer.

24. What will Oberon do with the special flower? What does he order Robin to do?

25. Choose the passage below that most appeals to you.

   2.1.2-15: The Fairy's description of wandering
   ("Over hill, over dale . . . And hang a pearl in every cowslip's ear.")

   2.1.91-117: Titania's description of the effects on the world of her and Oberon's "debate" ("Therefore the winds, piping to us in vain . . . By their increase now knows not which is which.")

   2.1.127-39: Titania's description of being with the Indian boy's mother
   ("His mother was a vot'ress of my order . . . As from a voyage, rich with merchandise.")

   2.1.161-74: Oberon's description of discovering the flower with special powers
   ("That very time I saw (but thou couldst not) . . . And maidens call it 'love-in-idleness'.")

   2.1.256-264: Oberon's description of where Titania will be sleeping
   ("I know a bank where the wild thyme blows . . . Weed wide enough to wrap a fairy in.")
   Weed means "garment" or "clothing" (*OED* 1, 2).

In the space below, make a list of key visual clues in your chosen passage, and then make a detailed illustration of it on the following blank page.

Your list of phrases with key visual clues:

Your illustration:

ACT 2, SCENE 2

1. The fairies sing a song to keep their sleeping Fairy Queen, Titania, safe (2.2.9-30). What are they trying to keep away from her? To whom are they speaking, for instance, when they command, "Come not near our Fairy Queen" (2.2.12)?

2. Second Fairy dismisses all of the fairies except one who is appointed to stand "sentinel" or guard: "Hence, away! . . . One aloof stand sentinel" (2.2.31-2). Oberon then approaches Titania to squeeze the magic flower juice into her eyes. If you were directing the play, how would you arrange for Oberon not to be stopped by the fairy "sentinel" or guard? Write a stage direction.

3. *Extra Opportunity* In what meter does Oberon speak when putting the spell on Titania? Consult appendix 1 on pages 94-98, and scan two lines:

   What thou seest when thou dost wake

   Do it for thy true love take. (2.2.33-4)

   Name of meter: _____

4. Reread Lysander and Hermia's conversation at 2.2.41-71 ("Fair love, you faint with wand'ring in the wood . . . With half that wish the wisher's eyes be pressed!").

   a. What reasons does Lysander give for asking to lie by Hermia's side?

   b. Lysander concludes with a play on the word "lie": "For <u>lying</u> so, Hermia, I do not <u>lie</u>" (2.2.58). *Lie* can mean reclining flat or telling a falsehood. Fill in the blanks below with your own words that explain what you think Lysander means by "lie" in each case:

   For _____ so, Hermia I do not _____.

   c. What reason does Hermia give for asking Lysander to "Lie further off" (2.2.63)?

5. Why does Robin put the love charm upon Lysander's eyes when he sees Lysander wearing "Weeds" (or clothes) "of Athens" and Hermia "sleeping sound" (2.2.76-85)? Clue: Robin concludes that Hermia dares "not lie / Near this lack-love" (2.2.83).

6. What feature of Hermia's does Helena describe after asserting, "Happy is Hermia" (2.2.96-7)? Fill in the blank:

   "For she hath blessèd and attractive _____."

   What do you think Helena means?

7. When Helena wakes Lysander, he says, "And run through fire I will for thy sweet sake" (2.2.109). What does Helena not understand about what now influences Lysander?

8. Lysander says:

   > Where is Demetrius? O, how fit a word
   > Is that vile name to perish[1] on my sword! (2.2.112-13)   [1] perish=to suffer death

   What does Lysander imply he will do to Demetrius? First, underline two words in the above passage that provide the biggest clues. Then, explain:

9. Lysander explains that "reason" has led him to love Helena even though before he had loved Hermia.

>The will¹ of man is by his reason swayed,
>And reason says you are the worthier maid. (2.2.122-3)

¹will=desire

Why might the audience of *A Midsummer Night's Dream* find Lysander's claim strange or funny that "reason" has made him love Helena? Has reason led Lysander to love Helena?

10. *Extra Opportunity* — Make an illustration of Lysander's two-part metaphor.

Reason becomes the marshal to my will
And leads me to your eyes, where I o'erlook
Love's stories written in love's richest book. (2.2.127-9)

11. What does Helena think is causing Lysander to be telling her he loves her? Clue: "Wherefore was I to this keen mockery born?" (2.2.130). (*Mockery* is ridicule; *keen* here means "bold" (*OED* 2).)

12. As Lysander abandons the sleeping Hermia, he speaks metaphorically about Hermia and his love for her. Analyze his first metaphor:

    For, as a surfeit¹ of the sweetest things   ¹*surfeit*=excessive consumption of food or drink (*OED* 1a)
    The deepest loathing² to the stomach brings, (2.2.144-5)   ²*loathing*=hatred

    vehicle   :   tenor

    surfeit of sweetest things :

    stomach   :

    The vehicle of Lysander's metaphor describes how eating too many sweet things brings a deep loathing, or hatred, to your stomach. What organ would he imagine was affected by loving too much? What does Lysander's metaphor imply is the effect of having loved Hermia so much?

13. As she wakes up, what is Hermia dreaming?

14. When Hermia wakes and realizes that Lysander is gone, she proclaims, "Either death or you I'll find immediately" (2.2.163). What might make Hermia feel so desperate? (Consider the choice Theseus presented to Hermia in act 1.)

☀ Act 2 Favorites ☀

Who is your favorite character in act 2?

What's your favorite phrase or line your favorite character says in act 2—either scene 1 or 2? Jot it down:

ACT 3, SCENE 1

1. At the rehearsal of their play, "Pyramus and Thisbe," Bottom proposes that he should speak a prologue to let the ladies know that "we will do no harm with our swords, and that Pyramus is not killed indeed" (3.1.18-19). If Bottom thinks that he must tell the ladies that they are not really going to do harm with their swords and that Pyramus—a character in the play—is not really killed, what must Bottom think about the ladies who will be watching the play?

2. Why does Bottom insist that Snug, who will perform the lion, must "tell them plainly he is Snug the joiner" (3.1.45)? (A *joiner* makes cabinets and furniture by joining wood.)

3. The play's script notes that Pyramus and Thisbe meet by moonlight, and Bottom and Quince puzzle over how "to bring the moonlight into a chamber" (3.1.47-8). What does their concern reveal about how they think a play script must be enacted? How do they solve the problem?

4. *Extra Opportunity* Do you think Shakespeare would have worried about bringing an actual source of light into a theater when a character speaks of moonlight? (Hint: review page vii of this guide.)

5. How does Bottom solve the problem of the needed wall?

6. *Extra Opportunity* In this scene Quince misuses a word when he suggests that an actor should say he "comes to disfigure, or to present, the person of Moonshine" (3.1.59-60). Why might this particular mistake—*disfigure* instead of *figure*—get a laugh?

7. Review the scene so far: what do the amateur actors' concerns indicate about how they imagine an audience experiences a play?

8. Robin asks, "What hempen homespuns have we swagg'ring here, / So near the cradle of the Fairy Queen?" (3.1.64-6). Robin refers to the working men by their home-made clothes of fabric spun from hemp—"hempen homespuns." What is Robin's attitude toward these working men?

9. Do you think Flute's performance of the part of Pyramus's lover, Thisbe, is well-acted? Start by quoting a phrase or two from which you derive your answer.

10. When Robin realizes that the men are rehearsing for a play, he remarks, "I'll be an auditor—/An actor too perhaps, if I see cause" (3.1.78-9). How does Robin become an "actor" in the play when Bottom exits?

11. Keeping in mind that Bottom seems not to realize what has happened to his head, what funny things does he say about his friends' reaction to his transformed state? Quote one or two lines.

12. What does Quince's "Bless thee, Bottom, bless thee!" suggest about what Quince thinks has caused Bottom to be "translated" (or changed) into a man with ass's head (3.1.120)? Why would Bottom need a blessing?

13. When Titania wakes and hears and sees Bottom, she remarks, "Mine ear is much enamored of thy note, / So is mine eye enthrallèd to thy shape" (3.1.140-1). Considering that Bottom has an ass's head, what has happened to Titania? (*Enthralled* means to be held captive; *shape* here means form or figure, that is, what Bottom looks like.)

14. When Titania tells Bottom, "I love thee" (3.1.143), how does Bottom respond? Fill in the blanks:

"Methinks, mistress, you should have little _____ for that. And yet, to say the truth, _____ and _____ keep little company together nowadays" (3.1.144-46).

In your own words, explain what Bottom says about reason and love:

15. ⁓ *Extra Opportunity* ⁓ Who has said something similar about love?

16. How does Bottom respond to Titania's compliments and declarations of love? Quote one or two key phrases. Then explain what these responses reveal about Bottom's character.

17. Choose what Bottom says to one of the faeries who serves him (either to Cobweb, Peaseblossom, or Mustardseed). Quote and explain it. How does Bottom treat his new servants? What does the way he treats them reveal about his character?

18. ✎ *Extra Opportunity* ✎ Titania orders the fairies attending her: "Tie up my lover's tongue. Bring him silently" (3.1.208). If you were directing the play, how would you stage this moment? What would Bottom be doing? How would the fairies tie up his tongue? Explain your idea either by writing a detailed stage direction or making a sketch of this moment in the scene.

ACT 3, SCENE 2

1. Reread Robin's (Puck's) description of how his mistress (Titania) came to be in love with a "monster" (3.2.6-36) and answer the following questions:

    a. What is Robin's attitude toward the men and toward the kind of work they do? He calls them, "A crew of patches, rude mechanicals, / That work for bread upon Athenian stalls" (3.2.9-10). (*Patch* means "fool" or "clown" (*OED* 1); *rude* can mean "slow-witted" or "uneducated" (*OED* 1b, 3); *mechanical* is an older name for someone who does manual work (*OED* A1, B1).)

    b. Analyze the simile with which Robin describes how Bottom's fellow-actors "fly" after Bottom is transformed to have an ass's head:

    > When they him spy,
    > As wild geese that the creeping fowler¹ eye,
    > Or russet-pated choughs², many in sort,
    > Rising and cawing at the gun's report³,
    > Sever⁴ themselves and madly sweep the sky.
    > So at his sight away his fellows fly⁵ (3.2.19-24)

    ¹*fowler* = a hunter of birds
    ²*chough* = a bird
    ³the *gun's report* would be the sound of the gun
    ⁴*sever* = part or separate
    ⁵to *fly* can mean to take wing or to run away

vehicle	:	tenor
geese or choughs	:	_____
fowler (and his gun's report)	:	_____
rise, caw, sever, sweep	:	_____
fly (take flight)	:	fly (run away)

53

c. Robin describes how the men's fear weakened their sense, which made it seem as if "senseless" (inanimate) things began to "do them wrong." He gives as an example: "For briers and thorns at their apparel snatch" (3.2.29-30), implying that the men experienced catching their clothes on thorns as if the thorns were purposefully snatching at them. Imagine you are the director and explain how the actors playing the men should act when a brier or thorn catches their "apparel" or clothing:

2. How does Oberon react to Robin's report? (Clue: "This falls out better than I could devise" (3.2.37).)

3. When Oberon and Robin see Hermia and Demetrius, what does Robin realize?

4. What does Hermia suspect Demetrius has done?

5. What does Demetrius mean when he calls Hermia, "the murderer" (3.2.62)? In what sense does he feel "murdered" by Hermia (3.2.60-3)? (Clue: with what, does he claim, has she "Pierced" his heart?)

6. ⚞ *Extra Opportunity* ⚟ Note how Hermia speaks to Demetrius: "Out, dog! Out, cur!" (3.2.67). Who else has used dog as a metaphor? Quote and cite the line, and compare the situations.

7. How does Hermia speak to Demetrius? Quote one or two lines and explain what they reveal about Hermia's feelings about Demetrius.

8. Why does Demetrius decide to stop following Hermia?

9. For what mistake does Oberon scold Robin? Quote the most important phrase in your answer.

10. What new command does Oberon give Robin?

11. When Oberon squeezes the magic love juice in the sleeping Demetrius's eyes, he says, "When his love he doth espy, / Let her shine as gloriously / As the Venus of the sky" (3.2.107-9). Who is "his love"? What does Oberon imply about why Demetrius has rejected Helena?

12. When Robin sees Helena and Lysander "Pleading for a lover's fee," he asks Oberon, "Shall we their fond pageant see" (3.2.116). *Pageant* is another word for a play. To what "pageant" does Robin refer? Sort the metaphor's vehicle and tenor.

    <u>vehicle</u>   :   <u>tenor</u>

    pageant   :   _____

    _____   :   Helena and Lysander

    What does this metaphor imply about Robin's attitude toward the mortal (human) world?

13. To what "sport" (3.2.121) does Robin look forward? (*Sport* here means "entertainment" (*OED* 1).)

14. What does Helena say about vows and oaths (3.2.133-6)? Sketch the image: "Your vows to her and me, put in two scales, / Will even weigh, and both as light as tales" (3.2.135-6).

15. When Demetrius wakes, he addresses Helena as "goddess, nymph, perfect, divine!" (3.2.140). He wonders to what he could compare her eyes, but says, "Crystal is muddy" (3.3.142). What does he mean?

16. How does Helena respond? What does she conclude Demetrius and Lysander both are doing? (Clues: "To conjure tears up in a poor maid's eyes / With your derision!" (3.2.161-2) and "all to make you sport" (3.2.164). *Derision* means ridicule or mockery; *sport* can mean entertainment.)

17. Lysander tells Demetrius, "In Hermia's love I yield you up my part" and asks Demetrius to "bequeath" to him his love of Helena (3.2.168-9). (*Yield* here means "to give as due" or "to give back" (*OED* 2, 4); *bequeath* means to announce that one is giving some possession to another person.) What does Lysander's declaration and request reveal about how he thinks of men's relationships with the women they love?

18. Analyze the metaphor with which Demetrius explains his love for Helena.

> If e'er I loved her, all that love is gone.
> My heart to her but as guest-wise sojourned[1],
> And now to Helen it home returned,
> There to remain. (3.2.173-6)

[1] *sojourn*="to make a temporary stay in a place" or "to be a lodger in another's house" (*OED* 1a,c)

vehicle	:	tenor
_____	:	my heart
guest-wise sojourned (*stayed temporarily*)	:	_____
home returned	:	_____
to remain	:	_____

19. ༺ *Extra Opportunity* ༻ Make a sketch of the metaphor.

20. When Lysander tells Hermia that "the hate" he bears her made him leave her, Hermia responds, "You speak not as you think. It cannot be" (3.2.196). What does Helena think "all three" (Lysander, Demetrius, and now Hermia) are doing to her (3.2.198)?

21. When Helena recounts for Hermia their "school days' friendship" (3.2.201-24), to what does she compare the two of them. Make a list:

22. ～ *Extra Opportunity* ～ Choose your favorite from the list above and sketch it.

23. Explain what Helena means when she concludes, "Our sex, as well as I, may chide you for it, / Though I alone do feel the injury" (3.2.223-4):

   a. What does Helena feel Hermia has done to injure her?

   b. Why might Helena feel that their "sex" (all women) would "chide" (scold) Hermia?

24. Does Hermia imagine, as Helena does, that Lysander is professing his love for Helena to scorn her? Quote and cite the line from which you derive your answer.

25. What does Lysander suggest he could do to prove to Demetrius his hate of Hermia?

26. Explain Hermia's questions, "Am I not Hermia? Are not you Lysander?" (3.2.285).

27. Once Hermia is convinced that Lysander does not jest but actually hates her, of what does she accuse Helena?

28. a. Jot down phrases that offer clues about Hermia and Helena's fight. (It starts when Hermia says to Helena, "O me! You juggler" (3.2.296)). What names, for instance, do they call each other? What clues can you find in their lines about what they are doing physically?

> b. ⚜ *Extra Opportunity* ⚜ Now, imagine you are directing the scene and write brief directions for the actors playing Hermia and Helena.

29. How does Helena eventually explain to Hermia why she told Demetrius of Hermia's secret departure from Athens—her "stealth unto this wood" (3.2.326)?

30. As you reread the instructions Oberon gives to Robin at 3.2.375-90 ("Thou seest, these lovers . . . with wonted sight"), make a list of important clues for:

   a. what the scene looks like

   b. how Robin acts

31. Why does Oberon want Robin to incite Demetrius and Lysander to fight?

32. Oberon gives Robin an herb to "crush . . . into Lysander's eye" and explains that the herb's "liquor hath this virtuous property, / To take from thence all error with his might / And make his eyeballs roll with wonted sight" (3.2.387-90). What does Oberon suggest here about why Lysander has been pursuing Helena? (*Wonted* means "customary, usual" (*OED* 11.3).)

33. What, according to Oberon, shall all the "derision" (ridicule, mockery) seem like to the lovers when they awake (3.2.391-2)? Fill in the blank:

"When they next wake, all this derision

Shall seem a _____ and fruitless vision."

34. Analyze the metaphor "fruitless vision":

    vehicle   :   tenor

    fruitless   :   _____

    <u>tree or plant</u>   :   vision

Do you think there are fruitful visions or dreams? If so, what metaphorical fruit do those visions or dreams bear?

35. While Robin is restoring harmony among the lovers, Oberon says, "I'll to my queen" (3.2.396). What is the purpose of his visit to Queen Titania?

36. Robin tells Oberon that they must act with haste because as the dawn, "Aurora," approaches, ghosts will be trooping home to churchyards. What evidence does Oberon give for his assertion, "But we are spirits of another sort" (3.2.410)? How are they different from the "damned spirits" Robin wants to avoid?

37. Review Oberon's instructions at 3.2.381-3 ("Like to Lysander sometime frame thy tongue. . . And sometime rail thou like Demetrius"). Then, write a stage direction for how Robin should say the following lines:

    "Here, villain, drawn and ready. Where art thou?" (3.2.424)   *stage direction:*

    "Ho, ho ho! Coward, why com'st thou not?" (3.2.448)   *stage direction:*

38. Once Lysander, Demetrius, Helena, and Hermia have decided to sleep for the night, Robin applies to Lysander's eyes the herb that Oberon has given him. What does Robin say as he does so (3.2.477-93)? Quote key words of his charm.

39. Note that Oberon does not order Robin to treat Demetrius's eyes with this error-correcting herb. What does Oberon's decision suggest is Oberon's view of Demetrius's love for Helena?

40. ~~ *Extra Opportunity* ~~ Review the charms with which Oberon and Robin anoint the eyes of Lysander, Titania, and Demetrius, and review those charms those with which they reverse the spells on Lysander and Titania. Note similarities and differences. What ideas do the charms suggest about sight and attraction?

✺ Act 3 Favorites ✺

What's your favorite fairy name? Circle it!

    Peaseblossom   Cobweb   Mote   Mustardseed

There are many rhyming lines in act 3. Jot down your favorite rhyme.

Which character would you most like to play in act 3? What would you wear as your costume?

ACT 4, SCENE 1

As you reread the opening of the scene, notice that Bottom doesn't seem to realize that he's been "translated" into a man with an ass's head and that Titania doesn't seem to realize that her new lover is a man with an ass's head.

1. Review what various characters say in the first fifty lines of the scene, and listen for clues about what Bottom looks like now: "Come, sit thee down upon this flow'ry bed . . . With coronet of fresh and fragrant flowers" (4.1.1-53). Imagine you are a costume and makeup designer. First jot down clues; then describe or draw a picture of your ideas for Bottom's costume and makeup design.

    Clues:

    Sketch or Description:

2. Choose one of the passages below, and write a detailed stage direction that suggests what the actors playing Titania and Bottom could do to help make the scene funny. Remember that actors should be reacting when they are not speaking.

Extra Opportunity Write a stage direction for both!

Titania Come, sit thee down upon this flow'ry bed,
While I thy amiable cheeks do coy,
And stick muskroses in thy sleek smooth head,
And kiss thy fair large ears, my gentle joy. (4.1.1-4)

stage direction:

Mustardseed What's your will?
Bottom Nothing, good monsieur, but to help Cavalery Cobweb to scratch. I must to the barber's, monsieur, for methinks I am marvels hairy about the face. And I am such a tender ass, if my hair do but tickle me, I must scratch. (4.1.22-7)

stage direction:

3. How does Bottom speak to the fairies that Titania has wait on him? What is his attitude toward his new servants? Start your answer by quoting one or two of Bottom's phrases or lines that provide the best clues.

4. As Oberon and Robin look on the sleeping Titania and Bottom, Oberon recounts meeting Titania and then gives Robin his next orders. Reread Oberon's speech at 4.1.47-71 ("Welcome, good Robin . . . But first I will release the Fairy Queen") and then answer the following according to Oberon's report:

   a. How does Oberon now feel when seeing Titania dote on Bottom (4.1.48-51)? Clue: "Her dotage now I do begin to pity." (*Dotage* means "foolish affection" (OED 2a).)

   b. Oberon says that the "dew, which sometime on the buds / Was wont to swell like round and orient pearls" was instead "Like tears that did their own disgrace bewail" (4.1.54-7). (*Sometime* here means formerly.) If dew used to look like pearls but now like tears, what does Oberon suggest is happening to the way the world looks while Titania is in love with Bottom?

   c. When Oberon asks for "her changeling child," Titania "straight" gave him to Oberon (4.1.60-3). If Titania gave up the boy so easily at this point, what can you infer makes her forget her previous fiercely felt obligation to the boy's mother?

d. What does Oberon announce that he will do now that he has the boy?

e. What does he instruct Robin to do?

f. What does Oberon plan for Bottom to think of all that happened during the night? Fill in the blank:

That he, awaking when the other do,

May all to Athens back again repair

And think no more of this night's accidents[1]   [1]accidents=events

But as the fierce vexation[2] of a _____. (4.1.67-70)   [2]vexation =disturbance

5. When Titania wakes, how does she understand her night with Bottom? Fill in the blank:

My Oberon, what _____ have I seen!

Methought I was enamored of an ass. (4.1.77-8)

71

6. Make a comic strip that illustrates Oberon and Titania's exchange about Bottom. Listen for clues about where Bottom must be. Stick figures are fine!

Titania	My Oberon, what visions have I seen!
	Methought I was enamored¹ of an ass. ¹*enamored of*=in love with
Oberon	There lies your love.
Titania	How came these things to pass?
	O, how mine eyes do loathe² his visage³ now! ²*loathe*=hate ³*visage*=face

(4.1.77-81)

My Oberon, what visions have I seen! Methought I was enamored of an ass.	There lies your love.
How came these things to pass?	O, how mine eyes do loathe his visage now!

7. How might Titania be feeling when Oberon shows her the sleeping Bottom, whom he calls "her love" (4.1.79)? With what tone might Titania ask, "How came these things to pass?" (4.1.76)? Give two possibilities.

8. a. What does Oberon tell Titania will happen "Now [that] thou and I are new in amity" (4.1.91-6)? (*Amity* means "friendly relations" (*OED*)).

   b. What does Oberon thereby suggest is the relationship between the fairy and the mortal worlds?

9. Why does Theseus call for the "Forester" (4.1.107)? What is he planning now that their "observation" (4.1.108) is performed?

10. ✎ *Extra Opportunity* ✎ Note how the transition between scenes is emphasized by a change of music. What kind of music had Titania called for (4.1.85)? What kind of "music" does Theseus look forward to (4.1.110, 114-15)? (Hounds are used in hunting.)

11. When Egeus wonders about the sleeping Hermia, Lysander, Demetrius, and Helena "being here together" (4.1.136), Theseus responds, "No doubt they rose up early to observe / The rite of May" (4.1.137-8). A bit later, Theseus greets young men and women by saying, "Good morrow, friends. Saint Valentine is past. / Begin these woodbirds but to couple now" (4.1.144-5). Do you think Theseus believes what he tells Hermia's father, Egeus? What seems to be Theseus's attitude toward the young people?

12. How does Lysander respond to Theseus's question, "How comes this gentle concord in the world" (4.1.149)? (*Concord* means harmony or peace.)

13. What does Egeus demand when he hears Lysander tell Theseus that he was intending to leave Athens? How, according to Egeus, would Lysander and Hermia's flight have "defeated" him and Demetrius (4.1.160-6)?

14. Demetrius speaks a metaphor and a simile to explain what happened to his previous love for Hermia. Analyze each figure by sorting its vehicle and tenor.

         my love to Hermia
Melted as the snow   (4.1.172-3)

<u>vehicle</u>   :   <u>tenor</u>

_____ : love to Hermia

melted   :   _____

      my love to Hermia . . .
        seems to me now   ¹ *idle*="void of meaning; foolish" (*OED* 2b)
As the remembrance of an idle¹ gaud²   ² *gaud*="a game, sport, or pastime" (*OED* 1a)
Which in my childhood I did dote³ upon (4.1.172-5) ³*dote*="to bestow excessive love on" (*OED* 3)

<u>vehicle</u>   :   <u>tenor</u>

_____ : love to Hermia

childhood   :   _____

If love can be like snow that melts or a childhood game one can lose interest in, what do Demetrius's metaphor and simile imply about being in love?

---

15. ~ *Extra Opportunity* ~ Demetrius then speaks a simile to explain how he now once again loves Helena, to whom he was engaged before he saw Hermia. Analyze the simile.

    The object and the pleasure of mine eye,
    Is only Helena. To her, my lord,
    Was I betrothed[1] ere I saw Hermia. [1]*betrothed*=engaged to be married
    But like a sickness did I loathe[2] this food. [2]*loathe*=hate
    But, as in health, come to my natural taste,
    Now I do wish it, love it, long for it,
    And will for evermore be true to it. (4.1.177-83)

vehicle	:	tenor
sickness	:	_____
loathe	:	_____
food	:	_____
health	:	_____
natural taste	:	_____

16. How does Theseus respond to what Demetrius and Lysander say? What does Theseus say to Egeus? What happens to the hunting plans? Where will they go "Three and three" (4.1.191)?

17. How do the lovers feel about what has happened? Review their conversation and quote two or three phrases that you think contain the most important clues.

18. What does Bottom's first line upon waking—"When my cue comes, call me, and I will answer" (4.1.210-11)—indicate about where he thinks he is and what he thinks is happening around him? (In a play a *cue* is the word that signals another actor to enter or begin to speak.)

19. When he fully wakes up, Bottom comments that he has had "a most rare vision" (4.1.214-5). What does Bottom decide about trying to explain his vision or dream with words?

20. Bottom decides that instead of speaking about his dream, he will get Peter Quince to write a ballad (a kind of song) of it. What reason does Bottom give that this ballad shall be called "Bottom's Dream" (4.2.225)?

21. Compare the reactions of those who wake up after the night in the woods—Titania, Lysander, Demetrius, Helena, Hermia, and Bottom. What does each say? Do you think Robin's idea that Bottom is particularly foolish—more so than the other mortals—holds true? Why or why not?

ACT 4, SCENE 2

1. When Quince asks if Bottom has "come home yet," Starveling responds, "Out of doubt he is transported" (4.2.1-4). Considering what has happened to Bottom, what does Starveling mean by "transported" here?

2. Why, according to the other men, "is the play marred" if Bottom "come not" (4.2.5)? (*Marred* means "ruined.") What do Quince and Flute say about Bottom?

3. Reread this part of the exchange about Bottom, and note Quince's mistake—*paramour* (a lover) instead of *paragon* (a perfect example or model):

    Quince [H]e is a very paramour for a sweet voice.
    Flute You must say paragon. A "paramour" is (God bless us) a thing of naught. (4.2.11-14).

    Consider what we, the audience, know about Bottom's recent adventures that his friends don't know. Then explain how Quince's mistake works as an inside joke for the audience of *A Midsummer Night's Dream*.

4. Snug remarks, "If our sport had gone forward, we had all been made men" (4.2.17-18). (*Sport* here means *entertainment*, namely the play they had been rehearsing.) What does he mean by "made men" (4.2.18)? What prompts Snug's remark? (Clue: Flute imagines the Duke would have given Bottom "sixpence a day for playing Pyramus" (4.2.22).)

5. When Bottom meets up with his fellow actors, what does he tell them about his experience since he last saw them? What does he not tell them?

6. When Bottom tells the men to get ready because the "Duke hath dined" and their "play is preferred," he orders, "let not him that plays the lion pare his nails, for they shall hang out for the lion's claws" (4.2.34-41). What does Bottom's direction reveal about his sense of how to represent a character in a play? (*Pare* means to cut or trim.)

7. Bottom then orders, "And most dear actors, eat no onions nor garlic, for we are to utter sweet breath, and I do not doubt to hear them say it is a sweet comedy" (4.2.42-4). Do you think Bottom is making a pun on "sweet"? If not, explain why not. If so, explain what two meanings of "sweet" are possible here. (*A pun is the use of a word in a statement that simultaneously suggests two or more meanings of the word and, thus, two or more ways to understand the statement.*)

❋ Act 4 Favorites ❋

Were there any lines in act 4 that made you laugh? What was your favorite line or phrase?

ACT 5, SCENE 1

1. The scene begins with Hippolyta remarking, "'Tis strange, my Theseus, that these lovers speak of" (5.1.1). What, before the scene begins, would "these lovers"—Demetrius, Helena, Lysander, and Hermia—have been speaking of?

2. Theseus asserts that what the lovers speak of is "[m]ore strange than true" (5.1.2). He compares lovers to madmen and poets as he explains why he doesn't believe their story. Answer the following questions according to what Theseus asserts in his speech at 5.1.2-23 ("More strange than true . . . How easy is a bush supposed a bear!"):

   a. If the imagination of the "lunatic, the lover, and the poet" are "all compact," what do they have in common (5.1.7-8)?

   b. How is the lunatic who "sees more devils than vast hell can hold" like the lover who "Sees Helen's beauty in a brow of Egypt" (5.1.9-11)? *(Note: Helen was a famous Greek beauty; Theseus implies that a woman from Egypt could not be as beautiful as Helen.)*

c. Theseus says that "as imagination bodies forth / The forms of things unknown, the poet's pen / Turns them to shapes and gives to airy nothing / A local habitation and a name" (5.1.15-18). In your own words, explain how Theseus describes what poets do. (A *habitation* is a place to live, a dwelling.)

d. Explain Theseus's assertion about "strong imagination": "That, if it would but apprehend *[feel emotionally]* some joy, / It comprehends *[grasps with the mind]* some bringer of that joy" (5.1.19-21)? How does Theseus suggest *feeling* joy can influence *thinking*? Hint: does Theseus seem to think there's necessarily a tangible "bringer" of the joy apprehended or felt?

e. Do you agree with Theseus? Can you think of a time when you felt joy without being able to identify a "bringer" of joy?

f. How can "imagining some fear" at night affect how a person perceives a bush (5.1.22-3)? Can you think of time your imagination transformed one object into another because you felt afraid?

g. How would you sum up Theseus's argument? Complete this sentence in your own words:

Theseus thinks lunatics, lovers, and poets are similar because they all _____

_____

_____ .

3. Is Hippolyta convinced by Theseus's disbelief of the lovers' stories? (Clue: She responds that "all the story of the night told over, / And all their minds transfigured so together" provide more evidence ("More witnesseth") than mere fantasy or imagination ("fancy's images") (5.1.23-6).)

4. Given what you've seen in *A Midsummer Night's Dream*, who do you think is more correct about what the lovers know and say—Theseus or Hippolyta? Start your answer by observing a specific moment in the play.

5. *Extra Opportunity* Theseus asks Philostrate what masques, dances, or music he has for the evening to "wear away this long age of three hours, / Between our after supper and bedtime" (5.1.34-7). He adds, "How shall we beguile / The lazy time, if not with some delight" (5.1.44-5)? What is Theseus's idea of what entertainment is for? (Clue: "lazy time" would pass slowly but could be tricked "beguiled" into moving faster with "delight" or entertainment.)

6. What is Philostrate's attitude toward the play "Pyramus and Thisbe" and the men who play it? How does Philostrate describe the play (5.1.65-74)? What does he say about the men (5.1.76-9)?

7. ⚞ *Extra Opportunity* ⚟ Theseus chooses the play despite Philostrate's critique of it and Hippolyta's reluctance. He explains how he has seen clerks "shiver and look pale" and "in their fears" not be able to speak their planned welcome before him, the Duke (5.1.101-5). Theseus explains:

   > Out of this silence yet I picked a welcome.
   > And in the modesty of fearful duty
   > I read as much as from the rattling tongue
   > Of saucy¹ and audacious² eloquence.   ¹saucy=rude ²audacious=daring
   > Love, therefore, and tongue-tied simplicity
   > In least speak most, to my capacity. (5.1.106-11)

   What, in sum, does Theseus say is more important than eloquent speech? What claim does he make about being able to understand intention when speech fails a fearful subject?

8. What is the purpose of the Prologue? (What had Quince and the other players most worried about when preparing to perform for the Duke?)

9. How do Theseus, Lysander, and Hippolyta respond to the Prologue? Quote one or two remarks and indicate with what tone you would direct the actor to say it.

10. Reread:

> *Theseus*   I wonder if the lion be to speak.
> *Demetrius*   No wonder, my lord. One lion may when many asses do. (5.1.161-2)

First explain what Demetrius means, and then explain what Demetrius doesn't understand his response would mean to the audience of *A Midsummer Night's Dream* that has just witnessed Bottom's transformation.

What Demetrius means:

What Demetrius doesn't realize that the audience of *A Midsummer Night's Dream* has witnessed:

11. Reread Snout's first speech (5.1.164-73), in which he announces that he "present[s] a wall" and explains that "This loam, this roughcast, and this stone doth show" that he is the wall through which the lovers Pyramus and Thisbe speak. Why would Snout think it necessary to give such an explanation before the action of the play begins? (*Loam* is clay; *roughcast* is plaster.)

---

12. ⚜ *Extra Opportunity* ⚜ Notice the rhyme and repetition in Bottom's first speech as Pyramus (5.1.179-93). How does the language of the play "Pyramus and Thisbe" compare to the language of *A Midsummer Night's Dream*?

13. Reread:

> Theseus The wall, methinks, being sensible, should curse again.
> Bottom No, in truth, sir, he should not. "Deceiving me" is Thisbe's cue. She is to enter now... (5.1.194-7)

Do you think Theseus intends his comment to be taken seriously? How does Bottom understand it?

14. a. Compare the lovers and events of the play performed by Quince and his men—"Pyramus and Thisbe"—to the lovers and events of *A Midsummer Night's Dream*. Jot down four or five comparisons in a chart below:

Lovers and Events in *MSND*	Lovers and Events in "Pyramus and Thisbe"

b. Consider your comparisons. What makes "Pyramus and Thisbe" have a tragic ending? What allows *A Midsummer Night's Dream* to avoid such tragedy?

15. *Extra Opportunity* Sketch Theseus's metaphor: "The iron tongue of midnight hath told twelve" (5.1.380). (As you plan your sketch, you might consider that in Shakespeare's day, clocks chimed on the hour.)

16. How does Robin describe "the time of night" (5.1.396-404)? Quote the parts of his description you find most striking.

17. Oberon and Titania, and their attending fairies, bless the house. Reread Oberon's blessing of the "bride-bed" and the "issue" (children) of the couples (5.1.418-39). What does the blessing aim to ensure about the married couples and their children? Start your answer by quoting key phrases.

18. Reread Robin's final speech, which is spoken to the audience of *A Midsummer Night's Dream*. It is at 5.1.440-55 ("If we shadows have offended . . . And Robin shall restore amends").

    a. How many times does Robin use the word "if" in this speech?

    b. What does Robin advise audience members to think "[i]f we shadows have offended" (5.1.440)? (In Shakespeare's day, *shadow* was another word for *actor*.)

c. For what does Robin imagine needing the audience's "pardon" (5.1.447)?

d. When Robin commands, "Give me your hands" (5.1.454), he likely is asking the audience to clap—to applaud. What does Puck promise in exchange for the audience's applause?

e. What does Robin's speech suggest about the relationship between actors and audience?

f. What does Robin say is "No more yielding but a dream" (5.1.445)? (Here *but* means "than"; *yielding* means "productive" (*OED* 2).)

g. By the end of *A Midsummer Night's Dream*, have visions and dreams yielded, or produced, anything? If so, what? And for whom?

☀ Act 5 Favorites ☀

Who is your favorite character in the play-within-the-play? Circle one and then briefly explain your choice.

    Pyramus   Thisbe   Wall   Moonshine   Lion

Who do you like more—the men performing the play "Pyramus and Thisbe" or the men who comment as they watch it? Briefly explain why.

LARGER QUESTIONS

Now that you have finished reading the play, you are ready to consider what the play as a whole might be suggesting about certain topics. Start by gathering passages about whichever topic you find particularly interesting.

1. **Eyes & Sight.** What do characters say about eyes? What powers do eyes have? Do characters talk about different kinds of sight?

2. **Love.** What do characters say about the nature of love? How do characters fall in love and become lovers? What do we learn about love between friends, such as Hermia and Helena or Titania and the Indian boy's mother?

3. **Marriage.** What do different characters say about marriage? How do they think marriages should be arranged? Which idea(s) of marriage seem to work out?

4. **Magic, Spells, & Charms.** What is Oberon's magic and how does it work? What about Robin's (Puck's)? What kinds of spells and charms do they speak? Who else uses or is said to use magic? What other than magic is said to be enchanting or bewitching?

5. **Change & Transformation.** Think about the many words used to describe change. (They include *transform*, *transpose*, *translate*, *transport*, and *transfigure*.) Who changes and by what are they changed? Which changes are considered normal? Which are considered unnatural or monstrous? At the play's end, who remains transformed? Who changes back?

6. **Dreams, Visions, & Shadows.** Only Hermia reports having a dream while sleeping. How does her dream relate to her waking life? What else do characters identify as dreams, visions, or shadows—or as like a dream? What, if anything, do characters think they can learn from dreams? What kind of dream is the dream of the play's title—*A Midsummer Night's Dream*?

7. **City (Athens) & Woods.** What happens in the city? What happens in the woods? What does the play suggest is the relationship between these locations?

8. **Reason & Imagination.** What do characters say and imply about how reason affects people? What do they say about imagination? What does the play overall suggest about reason and imagination?

APPENDIX 1. Listening to the Rhythms of Shakespeare's Poetry: An Introduction to Meter

Actors have long observed that Shakespeare's plays convey their meanings not only through the sense of his language but also through its sounds, including rhyme, alliteration (repeated consonant sounds), and assonance (repeated vowel sounds). As you read the play, read speeches aloud and listen for how the sounds contribute to their meanings. This section will help you get started listening for the rhythms of a Shakespeare play by introducing you to meters you will encounter in *A Midsummer Night's Dream*.

> ※ For most English literature, **METER** refers to a deliberate pattern of stressed and unstressed syllables.
>
> *"Stressed" syllables are the syllables that get the most emphasis when a word or sentence is spoken aloud.*
>
> *Keep in mind that you can hear the meter in which a poet has composed a speech or poem even while you can hear how the poet has, at times, varied that meter.*
>
> ※ In a Shakespeare play, speeches in **VERSE** are composed with a repeating pattern of stressed and unstressed syllables and are divided into deliberate lines. Shakespeare's verse is composed in meter.
>
> ※ In a Shakespeare play, speeches in **PROSE** are composed without a repeating pattern of stressed and unstressed syllables and are not divided into deliberate lines. Prose is not composed in meter.

Examples of VERSE in *A Midsummer Night's Dream*:

> HIPPOLYTA
> > Four days will quickly steep themselves in night;
> > Four nights will quickly dream away the time;
> > And then the moon, like to a silver bow
> > New-bent in heaven, shall behold the night
> > Of our solemnities. (1.1.7-11)

QUINCE
> Let Lion, Moonshine, Wall, and lovers twain
> At large discourse, while here they do remain. (5.1.159-60)

☀ *Quince's speech, two lines that have the same meter and that rhyme, is called a* **COUPLET**.

Notes about VERSE:

- When you are reading Shakespeare's verse, you will see that the first word of each new line of a speech is capitalized whether or not it begins a new sentence.

- Whatever the size of a book's pages, printers retain the lines of a speech in verse. Thus, often you will see empty space between the end of a line and the right margin of your book's page. If a line of verse is longer than what fits on a particular page, then what remains of the verse line usually is indented and printed directly below.

- When you quote verse, you should retain the capital letters and indicate the line breaks with a forward slash, called a *virgule*. Example: When Theseus complains that the time until their wedding is passing slowly, Hippolyta predicts, "Four days will quickly steep themselves in night / Four nights will quickly dream away the time" (1.1.7-8).

An example of PROSE in *A Midsummer Night's Dream*:

BOTTOM
> I see their knavery. This is to make an ass of me, to fright me, if they could. But I will not stir from this place, do what they can. I will walk up and down here, and I will sing, that they shall hear I am not afraid. (3.1.121-6)

Notes about PROSE:

- When you are reading prose, you will see that lines are printed until a word nearly reaches the right margin of the page. The first word of a new line, which varies depending on the size of the book, is not capitalized unless it happens to begin a new sentence.

❈ An **IAMB** is a poetic foot of one unstressed syllable (marked "˘") followed by one stressed syllable (marked "/"). Examples of single words that are iambs are:

˘ /   ˘ /   ˘ /
rehearse   consent   appear

❈ **IAMBIC PENTAMETER** names the meter of a line of verse with five ("penta") iambs. An example:

˘   /   ˘   /   ˘   /   ˘   /   ˘   /
The ox hath therefore stretched his yoke in vain, (2.1.96)

❈ **IAMBIC DIMETER** names the meter of a line of verse with two ("di") iambs. An example:

˘   /   ˘   /
But stay! O spite!
˘   /   ˘   /
But mark, poor knight, (5.1.291-2)

❈ *The above lines are another example of a COUPLET—two rhyming lines with the same meter.*

❈ Marking the stressed and unstressed syllables of a line of verse in the manner above is called **SCANSION**. To **SCAN** a line of verse is to listen for and mark its stressed and unstressed syllables and to notice what kind and how many of the repeating foot make up the line. Scansion also includes noticing any variations in the meter of a line. *(See page 98 for examples of variations in iambic pentameter.)*

➤ *EXTRA* ➤ Sometimes a line of verse is spoken by more than one character. Here is a single iambic pentameter line shared by Hermia and Helena:

˘   /   ˘   /
Hermia   Do you not jest?
                                        ˘   /   ˘   / ˘   /
Helena   Yes, sooth, and so do you. (3.2.276-7)

Note: Helena's speech is indented to show that it finishes Hermia's iambic pentameter line.

※ A **TROCHEE** is a poetic foot of one stressed syllable followed by one unstressed syllable. Examples of single words that are trochees are:

  / ˘   / ˘   / ˘
 mortal   fairy   moonbeams

※ **TROCHAIC TETRAMETER** names the meter of a line with four ("tetra") trochees. Examples:

 / ˘ / ˘ / ˘ / ˘
 If we shadows have offended,
  / ˘ / ˘ / ˘ / ˘
 Think but this, and all is mended: (5.1.440-1)

※ The above lines are another example of a COUPLET—two rhyming lines with the same meter.

 / ˘ / ˘ / ˘ /
 That you have but slumbered here
  / ˘ / ˘ / ˘ /
 While these visions did appear. (5.1.442-3)

> ⌒ EXTRA ⌒ The meter of these last two lines, which lack the unstressed syllable of their final trochee, is named **CATALECTIC TROCHAIC TETRAMETER**.

※ An **ANAPEST** is a poetic foot of two unstressed syllables followed by one stressed syllable. Examples of single words that are anapests are:

 ˘ ˘ /   ˘ ˘ /   ˘ ˘ /
 comprehend   undergo   overbear

☀ **ANAPESTIC DIMETER** names the meter of a line with two ("di") anapests. Example:

⏑ ⏑ / ⏑ ⏑ /
Over hill, over dale,
⏑ ⏑ / ⏑ ⏑ /
Thorough bush, thorough brier,
⏑ ⏑ / ⏑ ⏑ /
Over park, over pale,
⏑ ⏑ / ⏑ ⏑ /
Thorough flood, thorough fire; (2.1.2-5)

EXTRA Although much of *A Midsummer Night's Dream* is composed in iambic pentameter, you will hear many **VARIATIONS** in the meter. Below are two to listen for. When you notice a variation, consider what its sound adds to a speech's meanings.

☀ Some iambic lines end with an extra unstressed syllable. Such a line is said to have a **FEMININE ENDING**. An example of an iambic pentameter line with a feminine ending:

⏑ / ⏑ / ⏑ / ⏑ / ⏑ / ⏑
His mother was a vot'ress of my order, (2.1.127)

☀ Some iambic lines substitute a trochee for one of the iambs. Here's an example of an iambic pentameter line that begins with a **TROCHEE SUBSTITUTION**:

/ ⏑ ⏑ / ⏑ / ⏑ / ⏑ /
These are the forgeries of jealousy; (2.1.84)

APPENDIX 2. On How a Modern Edition of *A Midsummer Night's Dream* Is Made: Quarto & Folio

None of Shakespeare's handwritten play manuscripts has survived. Although Shakespeare was a member of the theater company that performed his plays, he was not involved in publishing the plays. Only after Shakespeare died were his collected plays published in a book entitled *Mr. William Shakespeares Comedies, Histories, & Tragedies*. This large book, called a *folio*, was first published in 1623. (Scholars now refer to this first edition of Shakespeare's collected plays as the *First Folio*.) While he was still alive, some of Shakespeare's individual plays were published in small books called *quartos*. A quarto of *A Midsummer Night's Dream* was published in 1600 and another in 1619, a reprint with minor changes. For most modern versions of the play, editors draw from the 1600 Quarto and the 1623 First Folio. If you are interested in the earliest copies of the play, you can find facsimiles of the them in your library or on the internet.[3]

Here are the first two lines of Helena's first soliloquy as they appear in the First Quarto and First Folio:

The 1600 "First" Quarto

Hele. How happie some, ore othersome, can be!
Through *Athens*, I am thought as faire as shee.

The 1623 "First" Folio

Hele. How happy some, ore othersome can be?
Through *Athens* I am thought as faire as she.

And here it is as printed in the 2016 Folger Shakespeare Library edition of the play at act 1, scene 1, lines 222-3.

> HELENA
> How happy some o'er other some can be!
> Through Athens I am thought as fair as she.

---

[3] Here are two websites that you might find particularly informative:
  The Shakespeare Quarto Archives at http://www.quartos.org/index.html
  Internet Shakespeare Editions at http://internetshakespeare.uvic.ca/Library/facsimile/

What differences do you notice between the early quartos and folio and your modern edition of *A Midsummer Night's Dream*?

- **Editors update spelling and punctuation.** So, for instance, the First Quarto's "shee" is now printed as "she," and "faire" is printed as "fair." (You also will notice that "shee" is spelled with a "long s," a letter no longer available among English fonts.)

- **Editors add stage directions not in the Quartos or First Folio.** Often editors distinguish their own stage directions from those in the early texts by enclosing them in parentheses or brackets. They base the stage directions they add on their understanding of the play, but you should feel free to imagine other possible stagings.

- **Editors mark act, scene, and line numbers.** Editors usually adopt the act and scene numbers marked in the First Folio, to which they add line numbers. Because some speeches in the play are in prose, not verse, a modern edition's line numbers vary depending on the size of the page. *(For explanations of* verse *and* prose, *see pages 94-95 of appendix 1.)*

- **Editors include notes that explain selected words and phrases.** In some notes editors provide definitions for words that might be unfamiliar to us now or whose meanings were different in Shakespeare's day. For instance, editors often note that the word *blood* in Theseus's advice to Hermia, "examine well your blood" (1.1.70), means *emotions, feelings, or passions.*

ACKNOWLEDGMENTS

Over the years I have had the pleasure of reading Shakespeare's plays with hundreds of students at Friends Seminary. Their enthusiastic interest in the plays, their willingness to work to understand them, and their fresh interpretations first inspired me to develop and publish guides to the plays. Exchanges with colleagues and students at other schools have encouraged me to continue the series. I am particularly grateful for having been welcomed as a guest teacher at the Taktse International School in Sikkim.

Lauren Simkin Berke has once again designed the cover for the guide: I continue to be thankful for Lauren's imaginative reading and exceptional craft. I also continue to be grateful to Robert Lauder, Principal of Friends Seminary, for his gracious support and to my colleagues for their enduring camaraderie and help. Heather Cross convinced me to make the guides available to the general public, made key suggestions about their structure, and responded generously to many questions. Chris Doire, Josh Goren, Philip Kay, Cara Murray, Thomas O'Connell, Katherine Olson, Phyllis Trout, and Craig Saslow have offered valuable comments as I developed the guides.

I am grateful to Donna Anstey at Yale University Press for permission to include an image of two lines scanned from the 1954 Yale University Press facsimile edition of *Mr. William Shakespeares Comedies, Histories, & Tragedies* and to Michael J. B. Allen for permission to include an image of two lines scanned from the University of California Press's 1981 facsimile edition, *Shakespeare's Plays in Quarto*, edited by Michael Allen and Kenneth Muir.

Years ago, Sarah Spieldenner and I worked together as we prepared to teach *A Midsummer Night's Dream* to middle-school students. My understanding of the play and my sense of how to help young readers experience it for themselves are rooted in my collaboration with Sarah. I am grateful not only for our ongoing exchanges but also for her specific suggestions about this guide. I remain thankful to Patrick Morrissey for his key advice about the guides; once again, he has read the manuscript with great care and offered vital suggestions. Final thanks are to Gordon Minette for help with matters large and small as I prepared *A Young Reader's Guide to Shakespeare's A Midsummer Night's Dream* for publication.

❈ NOTES ❈

❋ NOTES ❋

✺ NOTES ✺

NOTES

NOTES

NOTES

✺ NOTES ✺

www.ingramcontent.com/pod-product-compliance
Lightning Source LLC
Chambersburg PA
CBHW080445110426
42743CB00016B/3280